Explore Pandora

Editor Feyi Oyesanya
Project Art Editor Stefan Georgiou
Production Editor Marc Staples
Senior Production Controller Mary Slater
Managing Editor Emma Grange
Managing Art Editor Vicky Short
Publisher Paula Regan
Art Director Charlotte Coulais
Managing Director Mark Searle

Designed for DK by Colin Williams
Reading Consultant Maureen Fernandes

DK would like to thank Joshua Izzo and Rey Perez at Lightstorm and Nicole Spiegel at Disney.

First American Edition, 2026
Published in the United States by DK Publishing,
a division of Penguin Random House LLC
1745 Broadway, 20th Floor, New York, NY 10019

26 27 28 29 30 10 9 8 7 6 5 4 3 2 1
001–355817–Jun/2026

Published in Great Britain by Dorling Kindersley Limited

ISBN 979-8-2171-3984-2 (Paperback)
ISBN 979-8-2171-3985-9 (Hardcover)

Printed and bound in China

www.dk.com

This book was made with Forest Stewardship Council™ certified paper—one small step in DK's commitment to a sustainable future.
Learn more at **www.dk.com/uk/information/sustainability**

Level 2

Explore Pandora

Written by Feyi Oyesanya

DK

Contents

Welcome to Pandora

Pandora is a beautiful moon. This is where a species called the **Na'vi** live. They have blue, stripy skin and long tails. Pandora is filled with amazing wildlife.

At night, almost every living thing lights up.

The Rainforest

There are many rainforests on Pandora, with beautiful trees. The rainforests have many interesting animals and plants. They are all different shapes and sizes.

Tetrapteron

Panoprya
Celia fruit tree
Sturmbeest

Meet the Sully family

The Sully family are Na'vi. They live on Pandora. When the Resources Development Administration (RDA) return to Pandora, the Sullys must leave their home. Neteyam is the eldest child. He dies fighting in a battle. The Sully family miss him dearly.

Their human friend
Spider lives with
the family, too.
Neytiri
Neteyam
Kiri
Lo'ak
Tuktirey

The Omatikaya clan

The **Omatikaya** clan are very friendly. Family and friendships are important to them.

The Sully family used to live in the forest with the Omatikaya clan.

They love celebrating each other whenever they can, with music and food!

High Camp

High Camp sits in the mountains. It is hidden from the RDA. This is the new home of the Omatikaya clan and

the humans. They move after their old home is destroyed. They often cook around a campfire, sharing stories.

The Tree of Souls

Eywa is the spiritual goddess of Pandora. The Tree of Souls is where the Na'vi feel closest to Eywa. It is a large tree near

the mountains. This tree means a lot to the Omatikaya clan. They protect it as much as they can.

The Metkayina clan

The **Metkayina** are a Na'vi clan who live by the ocean. They live in peace with the ocean's

wildlife. The Metkayina clan teach the Sully family how to canoe, swim, and hunt at sea.

The Spirit Tree

The Metkayina clan visit the Spirit Tree to feel close to Eywa. It is deep in the ocean, so the Metkayina have to swim to get there. The tree can help them breathe underwater to keep them safe.

The Ocean

The ocean is filled with beautiful animals and plants. The Metkayina have a special

bond with creatures called **tulkun**. They call the tulkun their brothers and sisters.

The Tlalim clan

The **Tlalim** clan are also known as the Wind Traders. They fly around Pandora on large ships called gondolas.

They know Pandora well. The Wind Traders set up markets wherever they land and trade many things.

The Mangkwan clan

The **Mangkwan** clan believe that Eywa has turned her back on them. They cover

themselves with white and gray ash and are known as the Ash People.

Bridgehead

The RDA build a new city called Bridgehead. This city is for humans from Earth to move to.

Earth is getting more and more dangerous to live on. This is the human's last chance at survival.

Glossary

battle
a fight between groups

bond
a relationship between people or groups who share feelings, interests, or backgrounds

clan
a large group that live together and follow the same customs

goddess
a female god

Na'vi
a species native to Pandora. They are taller than humans and live in separate clans on different parts of Pandora

RDA (Resources Development Administration)
The RDA are humans who have traveled from Earth to take over Pandora

species
a group of animals or plants that are similar, live together, and create families

spiritual
feelings, thoughts, or beliefs that can bring peace

survival
the act of trying to live after a dangerous event or in dangerous situations

wildlife
animals and plants that live in nature

Index

NA'VI WORD PRONUNCIATION GUIDE

Eywa is pronounced EYE-WAH
Mangkwan is pronounced MANG-KWAHN
Metkayina is pronounced MET-KAH-YEE-NAH
Na'vi is pronounced NA-VEE
Omatikaya is pronounced O-MAH-TEE-KAH-YAH
Panoprya is pronounced PAH-NO-PREE-YAH
Tetrapteron is pronounced TEH-TRAP-TEH-RON
Tlalim is pronounced TLAH-LIM
Tulkun is pronounced TOOL-KOON

Quiz

Answer the questions to see what you have learned. Check your answers in the key below.

1. What color skin do the Na’vi have?
2. Who was Neteyam?
3. Where is the Spirit Tree?
4. What do the Metkayina clan call the tulkun?
5. How do the Wind Traders fly around Pandora?

Answers: 1. Blue 2. The eldest child in the Sully family 3. Deep in the ocean 4. Brothers and sisters 5. On ships called gondolas